One More Miracle

Embracing God's Daily Blessings

Marjorie L. Kimbrough

DIMENSIONS
FOR LIVING

NASHVILLE

ONE MORE MIRACLE
EMBRACING GOD'S DAILY BLESSINGS

Copyright © 2007 by Dimensions for Living

This book is printed on acid-free paper.

Library of Congress Cataloging-in-Publication Data

Kimbrough, Marjorie L., 1937-
    One more miracle : embracing God's daily blessings / Marjorie L. Kimbrough.
       p. cm.
    ISBN-13: 978-0-687-64291-5 (binding: pbk., adhesive, perfect : alk. paper)
    1. Miracles.   2. Devotional literature.   I. Title.
    BT97.3.K535 2007
    231.7'3—dc22

                                                                    2006033385

07 08 09 10 11 12 13 14 15 16—10 9 8 7 6 5 4 3 2 1
MANUFACTURED IN THE UNITED STATES OF AMERICA

For Dr. Karen Godette, a radiation oncologist,

who understands the real meaning of one more miracle

Contents

Introduction

Knowing that I had experienced many miracles in connection with my breast cancer, I was shocked when my doctor informed me that all we needed was one more miracle. With just one more miracle, I could consider myself cured. This information caught me off guard because I thought I was already cured. I had had the cancerous lump removed; I had undergone six weeks of radiation; I had taken tamoxifen for five years; and I had had several normal mammograms since then. I had been cancer free for seven years. What did she mean when she said that I needed one more miracle? When I raised that question, I was told that one has to be cancer free for *ten* years before one is considered cured. Although this news was somewhat disappointing, I know in my heart that God always has one more miracle. In fact, God has an unlimited supply of miracles. All I had to do was claim one of them! I had to believe without a doubt that whatever I was asking for, I would receive; I had to stand on God's promises. And that is what I did. I claimed God's promise of health and healing in my life. I did not give up; I embraced my faith. I expected my miracle.

I have been writing miracle stories for several years, and my doctor's comments led me to the writing of this book. There are many people who have needed and have received one more miracle. These are their stories. As you read them, remember that God always has another miracle. Claim it!

ANGELS

Do not forget to entertain strangers, for by so doing some people have entertained angels without knowing it.

—Hebrews 13:2

God's Everyday Angel

A hospice physician was driving home from a meeting when his car sputtered and died. He managed to coast into a gas station. Before he could call for a tow truck, he saw a young woman fall down as she came out of the building. He got out of his car to offer help, but as he approached her, he saw that she had not fallen but was simply sitting down on the ground, sobbing. When the doctor spoke with the woman, he found out that she was traveling to another state with her three children and that she had just spent her last five dollars on gas. At the price of gas, five dollars had gotten her only two gallons. She did not know how she would make it any farther.

The doctor asked if she had been praying, for he felt that God had sent him in answer to her prayers. He used his credit card to finish filling up her gas tank and went to the adjacent fast-food restaurant to purchase food and gift certificates for the children. He discovered that she was on her way to stay with her parents because she knew she could not pay next month's rent. Her parents had said that she and the children could stay with them until she could find a job and gain some stability.

Feeling that he had done all he could do for the woman and

her children, the doctor started toward his car to call the tow truck. As he was leaving, the woman asked if he was an angel. He replied that angels are very busy and sometimes God uses regular people.

When the doctor got back in his car, he thought he would try to start it just for fun. Of course, it started right away. He knew then that there had never been anything wrong with it. God just needed him to help with a miracle.

God always has another miracle. Claim it!

Lord, I want to participate with you in someone's miracle. Amen.

A Newborn's Miracle

A young mother had just given birth in Indonesia. The baby was very tiny, being just one-third the normal birth weight. The newborn was taken to the hospital's nursery and was placed in an incubator. Shortly after the birth, the mother and father heard a terrible rumble. Remembering the tsunami of a few months earlier, they knew that they needed to seek higher ground. They could not make it to the nursery, and so they prayed that someone would get their baby and bring her to safety.

Although it was difficult for the new mother to move through the rubble and falling debris that the earthquake was causing, she and her husband managed to get to higher ground. They were relieved to discover that they were experiencing an earthquake and not a tsunami, but they did not know where their baby was. As soon as it was safe to return to the place where the hospital had stood, they returned. Among the rubble that once was a hospital they found an incubator, but no baby. The mother was devastated, but her husband insisted that God would provide for their baby because of her innocence. He said that she was without sin and would be protected.

Four days later a nurse was looking for the parents of a tiny newborn. She had taken the baby with her to what remained of her home, had kept the baby warm with her own body, and had fed her powdered milk. The parents were so elated and grateful that they decided to name their baby after that nurse. They knew that they had experienced a miracle.

God always has another miracle. Claim it!

Holy Father, we are so grateful for those who were saved during the earthquakes and tsunamis. May they live their spared lives in service to you. Amen.

The Miracle of Anticipation

Bob was in a small hospital in Europe, and he was in severe pain following his operation. He could hear the sounds of others who were also experiencing pain. It was after midnight, and he didn't want to call for the nurse; but he wondered if he really had a choice. His bedding was a mess, he could not get back to sleep, and the snores of his roommates were driving him crazy. He questioned whether he was putting unreasonable standards on such a small hospital in a foreign land. Perhaps they were doing the best they could and did not have sufficient staff to attend to his personal needs.

He stood the discomfort as long as he could. Just as he was about to reach for his call button, the nurse appeared. She brought tea, a cold pack for his wound, and earplugs. She even said that she would move him to an empty room away from the snorers. How had she known his distress?

Without asking him what he needed, the nurse remade his bed, gave him some painkillers, poured his tea, and emptied his urinal flask. She looked around to see what else she could do. Then she fluffed up his pillow, brought him a towel, treated his stitches, gave him a tranquilizer, and wished him a good night. Was she a mind reader?

Bob could not believe her kindness. Then he thought about God. God answers before we call and does more than we can ask or think. The nurse had done the same thing. It was a miracle of anticipation, and the nurse surely was an angel.

God always has another miracle. Claim it!

Lord, thank you for always doing abundantly more than we can ask or imagine. Amen.

A Miracle Race

Every year on the Fourth of July, Atlanta clears its famous Peachtree Road for the Peachtree Road Race. It is a 6.2-mile race that averages over fifty-five thousand participants. Although I have never even suggested that I might enter the race, my husband says that one day he will be among the participants. There are both runners and walkers in the crowd, and everyone tries to cross the finish line and win the coveted T-shirt. My husband actually got a T-shirt one year, but not because he ran and finished the race. He was selected to pray for the runners before the race began.

One year there was a participant, Don Plunkett, who suffered a nearly fatal heart attack during the fifth mile of the race. Although Don had run in the race in years past, this time he was walking. He collapsed right in the midst of other runners and walkers, but God was there. God sent his runner Carla to begin CPR. Then God summoned his doctor Lee, an anesthesiologist, to help Carla. God also sent his runner Rhonda to lead the crowd that had gathered in prayers for Don's recovery. Any of these runners could have kept running, but God had directed them to just the place where Don needed them.

Although Don does not remember the fall or the CPR that was administered, he is grateful that Carla, Lee, and Rhonda were in place. He remembers waking up in the ambulance accompanied by Lee. Lee ended his race and the prospect of his T-shirt when he responded to Don's need. He was there when the paramedics shocked Don with a defibrillator to restore his heartbeat. The defibrillator paddles left burn marks on Don's chest, but he is so proud of them. The race director even left a T-shirt for Don at the hospital; and although Don promised to give that T-shirt to Lee, the director delivered one to Lee as well.

Don is convinced that his survival was a miracle of God. God used everyone he needed to make Don's miracle a reality. Don is now a strong CPR advocate and has vowed to recruit his neighbors to learn the lifesaving skill. He knows that God miraculously saved him for a few more months or years, and he hopes to use this extended time wisely.

God always has another miracle. Claim it!

Lord, thank you for your "angels" who are with us in our time of need. Amen.

The Inner Voice Miracle

Have you ever heard that little inner voice that tells you to do something—or even not to do something? Well, Tony heard it. He and his wife had just sat down to eat when that little inner voice told him to go see his neighbor right away. He tried to ignore it, but it persisted. To his wife's dismay, he left the table and went to see his neighbor.

When he arrived at his neighbor's house, he could not get anyone to answer the door. Again, that little inner voice told him to try the back door. It was open, so he called out to his neighbor as he entered. He heard a cry coming from another room and found his neighbor on the floor, unable to move. She looked at him and asked where he had been and why it had taken him so long to get to her house. Tony did not understand what she was talking about, and he began to get an attitude, thinking that she ought to be grateful that he had come at all. But she ignored his attitude and continued her chastisement of him by explaining that she had been praying for him to come for half an hour.

Because Tony was obedient to that little inner voice, he became the answer to his neighbor's prayer. After she had fallen, she had had no idea how she would get up. She had listened to a little inner voice that had told her to pray that God would send Tony to assist her. God had answered her prayer by telling Tony what to do through a little inner voice.

I wonder how many times we have missed our miracles or our opportunities to be miracle workers by failing to listen to that little inner voice. We are God's miracle workers, and God always has another miracle. Claim it!

Lord, open my ears so that I may hear your voice within. Amen.

Unexpected Success

While I was shopping in the grocery store, a woman stopped me and asked if I would check the list she was holding against the items she had in her shopping cart. I could tell by the broken English she was using and by the hesitancy with which she approached me that she was mentally challenged. I assumed that she was given the task of making a list and shopping by herself to prove that she could successfully accomplish that task alone. (I am familiar with some group homes that care for those who are mentally challenged and teach them survival skills.)

I looked at her list and noticed that she had badly misspelled the several items she had already picked up, but I could tell what she meant. There was one item missing. Her list read "Hell may." I immediately knew she meant Hellmann's Mayonnaise. I told her that she did not have the mayonnaise, and she smiled and said, "I do real good. I only forget one thing." I said, "Yes, you did very well. I am so proud of you!" She was overjoyed, for she felt she had been successful.

I was deeply touched by this experience. I wondered why, of all the shoppers in the store, this woman decided to ask me for help. I also wondered what her response would have been if she had not been affirmed and congratulated. Then I remembered that miracles happen every day. I know it was God who directed her to me because she needed affirmation, and I was in place to give it.

It is a miracle that God has directed persons to work in homes for those of his children who are mentally challenged. It is a miracle that those residents boldly venture out into a world where they are considered different and even inferior. And it is a miracle that there are children of God ready and willing to assist when called upon.

God always has another miracle. Claim it!

Lord, enable me to assist in your daily miracles. Amen.

A Child Leads

A family consisting of a mother, a seven-year-old son, a four-year-old daughter, and a two-year-old daughter was traveling home from dinner with friends. The mother knew that it was getting late, so she dressed her children for bed before leaving her friend's house. On the way home, the mother lost control of her car and ran off the road. All three children were wearing their seat belts and were unharmed; however, the mother was thrown from the car and suffered several injuries.

The seven-year-old boy managed to get out of the car to look for his mother, but because it was dark, he could not find her. He knew that he had to get help for his lost mother and his sisters, so he talked to his sisters and told them that he had to go to get help. He asked the four-year-old to take care of the two-year-old, and he told them not to be afraid. He did not mention that he was afraid of the dark, but somehow he knew that God would take care of him.

Walking almost a mile in footed pajamas, the boy came to a farmhouse. He heard voices and knocked on the door. He begged the occupants to go with him to help his mother and sisters. They returned with him to the site of the accident.

They found the mother on the side of the road. She was hospitalized, and the doctors said that in all probability, the little boy had saved his mother's life. He had proved to be a real hero. He had taken charge of the situation. He had provided as best he could for his sisters by calming their fears and promising to return with help. He had suppressed his own fears of the dark and had ignored the fact that he had to walk without shoes. I know the Holy Spirit led him, and it was a miracle.

God always has another miracle. Claim it!

Lord, I pray for all the children who sometimes have to assume adult roles. I thank you for leading them. Amen.

Angels in the Midst

One sunny day a football coach just happened to be driving by a marina at the exact time that another man had a seizure and drove into the water. The coach did not know that the man had had a seizure, and he did not know how he could help. But he did know that his help was needed. Almost without thinking, he got out of his car and dove into the water. He was a strong swimmer, and he just prayed that he would be able to figure out how to rescue the man. He did not know whether or not he would be successful, but he knew that he had to try. He managed to pull the man from the submerged vehicle and get him ashore. Then he retrieved his cell phone and arranged for emergency care. The real miracle was that he just happened to be passing by at the exact time the man had the seizure and lost control of his car.

On a different day in a different city, a woman was driving along a busy expressway when she was hit by a sport utility vehicle. That accident knocked her into a pickup truck, but her precarious journey did not end there. The pickup truck knocked her into the path of a public bus. Just think: This poor woman had been knocked around by a sport utility vehicle, a pickup truck, and a bus; yet, she survived. Her only injuries were multiple breaks to her wrist and hand.

Perhaps that football coach was God's designated angel, and perhaps an invisible angel protected the woman on the expressway. I don't know. But I do know that God always has another miracle. All we have to do is claim it!

Lord, we are daily surrounded by your acts of grace and mercy, and we are grateful. Amen.

BLESSINGS

And God is able to make all grace abound to you, so that in all things at all times, having all that you need, you will abound in every good work.

—2 Corinthians 9:8

The Thirty-One-Cent Miracle

Frank had been unemployed for eight months. He tried desperately to balance looking for a job and staying afloat. He did odd jobs for neighbors and relied on his pastor and church members to help him in times of dire need. He had to decide between paying the electric bill and paying the gas bill. The electric bill won. But because the heat and the hot water were gas dependent, Frank had to live in a cold apartment and take cold showers.

Frank did what he could to search for a job. He tried networking, the Internet, and the newspapers. He went to see his pastor and was advised to change his approach. His pastor advised him to start expecting a miracle, to expect God to provide. Frank thought about this advice and prayed for a miracle.

At long last Frank found a company with a need he was qualified to fill, but the company took its time about hiring. He had to endure several interviews and was told that he would be hired in a couple of months. Frank knew that he could not wait that long. His gas tank was on empty, and he had a total of thirty-one cents in his pocket.

Frank's suffering had made him strong. Feeling that he had nothing to lose, he decided to tell the managing director, who had the power to hire, that he could not wait two months. He had bills to pay, food to buy, an empty gas tank to fill, and only thirty-one cents left to spend. The director was impressed not only with Frank's honesty but also with his skills. He gave Frank a check for $10,000, which was to be considered a signing bonus. He was to report to work immediately. Frank knew that if he thanked God and his pastor every day all day, it would not be enough.

Frank went to the interview with thirty-one cents and left with a job and $10,000.31. It was a miracle!

God always has another miracle. Claim it!

Father God, thank you for supplying all our needs. Amen.

Learning from Tragedy

In recent years, several families have lost young athletes to previously undetected heart conditions. As a result of these deaths, a special heart-screening test program called Heart Screens for Teens was developed. This heart screen was used to detect a hole in the heart of Tricia McCue, a seventeen-year-old high jumper. Although Tricia's track career is over, her family is grateful that the defect was discovered.

Tricia's story makes us aware of the blessings God has in store for us. Like the several athletes who had already died,

Tricia had no alarming symptoms. Sometimes she had suffered from shortness of breath, but she was not concerned. She thought that what she was experiencing was the normal result of extending herself in preparation for competition. She was not even going to take the heart-screening test; but after her mother heard about the other teens who had died, she insisted that Tricia be screened. Her mother remembered that several years ago they had discovered that Tricia had a non-threatening heart murmur.

After administering the echocardiogram and considering both the heart murmur and the shortness of breath, the problem with Tricia's heart was located, and surgery was ordered.

Although Tricia realizes that high jumping and track are no longer a part of her life, she is very enthusiastic about helping coach and manage the jumpers at her school. In this way she stays close to the action.

Both Tricia and her mother are grateful to the family of Ryan Boslet for their persistence in pushing a bill through the state House that would mandate a state-wide standardized physical for all athletes in sixth grade through twelfth grade. Ryan was one of the young athletes who lost his life due to an undetected heart condition. His family suffered a tragic loss, but from that tragedy Tricia's miracle emerged.

God always has another miracle. Claim it!

Lord, help us learn from the tragedies in our lives. Amen.

A Lifesaving Phone Call

Ralph is eighty years old, and he loves to sing. He has been singing with a community chorale group for several years, and he enjoys being the soloist for several of their numbers.

The chorale group was scheduled to sing for a local prison, but Ralph was having chest pains and was advised to have bypass surgery. Reluctantly, Ralph called his chorale director and told her that he would not be able to sing for the prison. The director understood his health needs and promised to stay in touch throughout his recovery.

The group sang at the prison and even told the inmates that Ralph was disappointed that he was not able to be with them.

Knowing that Ralph lived alone, the director called him after his surgery to see how he was doing. He told her that he was very tired. Then his speech became slurred, and he was only able to make grunting sounds. The director's husband had previously had a stroke, and she felt certain that Ralph was having one. She used her cell phone to call 911 while she kept Ralph on the line. The 911 operator told her that they needed an address. In her frustration, she could not find her address book, but she enlisted her daughter to help. They finally found the address book and relayed the address to the 911 operator.

Ralph had, indeed, had a stroke, but he was transported to the hospital before he succumbed. He cannot speak and is partially paralyzed, but his family is so grateful that he was talking to his director when the stroke occurred. It was a lifesaving phone call.

God always has another miracle. Claim it!

Lord, thank you for friends who care about us and appreciate what we do in ministry to others. Amen.

The Miracle of Sharing

I first met Serena when she came to the hospital to visit her uncle. She was a beautiful child and very polite for a four-year-old. Her grandmother, who was with her, told me the story of Serena's birth to a mother who was a drug addict. As a loving grandmother, she had assumed the care of Serena, but she was unable to provide all of the clothes and other amenities that she wanted Serena to have. She also said that she would willingly and gladly take hand-me-downs. Knowing that I had friends with children in the same age category, I asked what size clothes she needed. Upon hearing her answer, I promised to have some nice things for Serena in short order.

I called one of my adopted daughters, who is the mother of two girls just a little older than Serena, and I asked if she had any clothes in the size that Serena needed. Of course, she had plenty of them, and she promised to clean them and bring them to me. She did just that, bringing some beautiful clothes to my house.

I called Serena's grandmother and told her what I had. She and Serena came over to pick up the clothes. I wish you could have seen the smile on Serena's face. She did not expect to see the beautiful clothes that were now hers. Her grandmother was in tears and just could not say enough thank-you's.

What a simple thing to do: make a few contacts and arrange for Christian people to help one another. What a blessing, and what a miracle!

God always has another miracle. Claim it!

Lord, thank you for giving us hearts that are willing to share our blessings with others. Amen.

The Fire Ant Miracle

Pat and her husband and children were returning from a church conference when a tire on their car exploded. The car skidded off the road and collided with a tree. Although her son and daughter were not badly hurt, Pat had torn ligaments in her right knee, and her husband was unconscious. She and her daughter decided to go for help while her son stayed with his father.

Pat could not find her cell phone and could barely squeeze through the car door that would open only a few inches. Her daughter ran up the road to signal for help, but Pat had to crawl. Her knee was painful and swelling. She tried to keep her daughter in sight and instructed her to stay out of the middle of the road. All she could do was sit in the grass while her daughter waved her hands in hopes that someone would see her and stop.

Finally, a car stopped. The driver asked what had happened and if anyone was hurt. Pat explained that her husband needed medical attention and that her knee was killing her. The woman who was driving the car used her cell phone to call for aid. In short order, an ambulance arrived and transported the family to the hospital.

Pat's husband was badly injured, but his injuries were not life threatening. Pat was so relieved to hear her husband's good news that she almost missed noticing her own miracle. There were tiny red bumps all around her swollen knee. She had been sitting in a bed of fire ants as she waited for help on the side of the road. Their bites had prevented a potentially fatal blood clot from forming. God had placed those fire ants in just the right place with just the right assignment. It was a miracle!

God always has another miracle. Claim it!

Lord, you use every one of your creatures to assist in performing miracles. Thank you! Amen.

An Unexpected Blessing

Dylan was one of the many high-tech professionals who lost his job after a downturn in the economy. He was out of work so long that his unemployment benefits ended. Although his wife, Susan, was working, her salary alone was not enough to cover the bills, food, lodging, and other expenses. Dylan spent his days and part of his nights looking for a job. He went on interviews and found that either he was overqualified or there just were no openings. He told Susan to keep praying.

While Susan was being faithful in praying for a job for Dylan, a friend called to ask if Susan would pray for her family. Neither that friend nor the friend's husband had a job, and they had children to support. Although Susan knew that she could not afford to help her friend, she felt compelled to do so. She discussed the situation with Dylan, and they decided to give her friend enough money to buy groceries for a few days. Their action would mean that they would have to cut their own expenses somewhere. Perhaps they could delay paying a bill or buy less food or somehow stretch what little money they had. No matter what they had to do, they knew that God expected them to help their friends.

By the next week, when their resources were almost all gone, Dylan found a job. They knelt in prayer, believing that their sacrificial gift had been rewarded with the miracle of a job.

God always has another miracle. Claim it!

Lord, give us the courage to be obedient to your call for sacrificial giving. Amen.

The Miracle of Rain

After having lived through several very dry summers, I can relate to the droughts that often occur in farmlands. I have been told of a miracle that brought rain to a parched earth.

Mary and her husband made daily trips to a water rendering plant in an effort to get water to their fields. They knew that the water supply was becoming depleted and that without rain their crops would die. As Mary prayed for rain, she noticed her six-year-old son walking toward the woods as still as possible, with his hands cupped in front of him. After a brief time, he ran out of the woods only to cup his hands and walk with great care back into the woods again. He kept making this trip for over an hour.

Mary's curiosity got the better of her, and she decided to follow her son into the woods. She was careful to stay out of sight, thinking that he probably did not want her to see what he was doing. She noticed that by cupping both hands in front of him, he was careful not to spill a drop of the water that he had collected from a hose.

He was taking the water to a dehydrated and heat-exhausted fawn, which lay surrounded by older deer. None of the older deer approached the boy. They knew he was trying to help. As the fawn lifted its head to lap the precious water, the boy beamed with pride.

Mary was so proud of her son and his efforts to save the tiny fawn. She got a small pot of water from the kitchen and joined her son on his return to the woods. She did not try to approach the fawn; she let her son do it. The deer knew him. She stood at a distance and watched while her son gave a drink to his tiny friend.

Mary's eyes filled with tears of joy and pride. Her son was showing such great love. Her emotions soared, and as tears dropped from her eyes, rain dropped from the sky. God's tears had joined hers, and he had sent the miracle of rain!

God always has another miracle. Claim it!

Lord, thank you for the loving hearts of children. Help us always remember that unless we become like children, we shall not enter your kingdom. Amen.

The Miracle Gift

Six-month-old Rachel desperately needed the gift of new lungs. She had been struggling for months to stay alive, but her lungs were failing. Her parents and physicians made a national plea for a donor set of lungs. Without new lungs, she would surely die.

Did her parents and physicians even know what they were asking for? Rachel was a tiny baby and needed a baby's lungs. Some other baby would have to die so that Rachel could live. Would it even be possible for a six-month-old baby to survive the kind of surgery required for a lung transplant?

The only thing her parents and physicians knew was that Rachel had a condition known as alveolar dysplasia, which, together with her pulmonary vascular disease, meant that she had too few air sacs to breathe normally. The air sacs she did have did not work properly; trying to breathe not only required tremendous energy but also put pressure on her heart and other organs. Rachel needed a miracle gift of donor lungs.

Although the organ bank would not say where the lungs came from out of respect for the donor family, Rachel got her miracle. She was in critical condition following the surgery, but she tolerated the surgery well.

Prior to the surgery, Rachel's physical and mental development was adversely affected; but after the surgery, her development was expected to be normal. She was blessed to receive a miracle gift.

God always has another miracle. Claim it!

Lord, keep us mindful of the need for organ donations. Someone may need that miracle gift. Amen.

A Miracle of Generosity

Each year the Higher Education Ministry at Cascade United Methodist Church in Atlanta, Georgia, sponsors a scholarship awards program. During that program, scholarships are awarded to students entering or returning to college. Some of these students are members of the church; but because of the church's desire to extend its mission and be a light in the community, some students are nonmembers.

I am so happy that Cascade has this vision. In addition to scholarships that are budgeted by the church, various groups within the church also offer scholarships. Some of the groups offer scholarships in memory or in honor of their members; some choirs offer scholarships to students planning to major in music; some individuals offer scholarships to students planning to attend their alma maters; and some members who belonged to sororities and fraternities offer scholarships to deserving applicants. The applicants do not have to belong to the groups awarding the scholarships. This type of community inclusion is considered a part of Cascade's outreach ministry. Numerous scholarships are awarded, and it is a glorious giving ministry.

This year the money awarded to students exceeded $170,000. This amount was a milestone. We all rejoiced in having reached it, but our pastor will not allow us to be satisfied with this milestone! Our next goal is to exceed $250,000. Can you imagine a church awarding a quarter of a million dollars in scholarships? Can you even imagine a church with a no–fund-raising policy awarding scholarships exceeding $170,000? It is truly a blessing and a miracle of giving.

God always has another miracle. Claim it!

Lord, thank you for people who not only are grateful for their blessings of education and finances, but also are willing to share them with others. Amen.

The LASIK Miracle

During a routine physical at the age of seven, it was determined that my older son needed glasses. I took him to an ophthalmologist, and he was fitted for glasses. The morning after he got his glasses, he walked outside and announced in total surprise, "Mom, I can see across the street!" He did not know that most people could see across the street without glasses.

Wearing glasses was second nature to him for twenty-seven years, but then he became increasingly concerned that his eyes were steadily deteriorating. He decided to have laser vision correction. During this procedure, a computerized excimer laser is used to remove a thin layer of tissue from the cornea. This flattens the cornea to the desired correction so that the eye can focus properly. The pulses of light emitted from the laser surgically reshape the surface of the cornea using the same principles that eyeglasses and contact lenses use.

It is simply overwhelming to consider how God has designed our eyes and vision and to see that man has developed the intelligence to mimic what God has done throughout creation. For God, this process is natural; for man, it is a miracle!

My son's surgery was successful. He was able to see without his glasses immediately following the procedure. He wore sunglasses to cut down on the glare, and he filled a prescription for eyedrops so that he would not strain his eyes during the next few days. The morning following the surgery, he drove himself to the doctor for a checkup. The doctor was amazed by the amount of healing that had already taken place. Just the day before, my son would not have been able to see well enough to attempt to drive around the corner without his glasses.

Thinking that he would probably need a reduced prescription

for his glasses, my son asked the doctors for one. They informed him that he no longer needed glasses at all. He was shocked! Still, because he was so used to wearing his glasses, he asked that clear lenses be put in his frames. The LASIK miracle was greater than he had dared imagine!

God always has another miracle. Claim it!

Lord, thank you for the intelligence that allows men and women to scratch the surface of your miraculous design of the human body. Amen

God's Miraculous Supply

Patricia was divorced and caring for her two young sons. Although the boys were very young, they had big appetites; and Patricia had very little money. She depended on her ex-husband to send child support, but he very rarely sent it.

One day when the food supply was very low, the only thing Patricia could offer her sons for dinner was a sandwich. After they had eaten their sandwich, they asked what was for dinner. She told them that they had eaten it. The boys complained that they were still hungry. Patricia did not know how she could satisfy their hunger; all she knew to do was pray. She got down on her knees and told God all about her problems. She asked for direction and for funds to buy what her boys needed to satisfy their hunger.

Even before Patricia had finished praying, there was a knock on the door. She got up to answer it and found some neighbors with fresh vegetables and fruit from their garden. They told her that they had much more food than they could eat and that they wanted to share some with her and her sons. Patricia was overcome with praise and thanksgiving. She immediately began to cook the vegetables and wash the fruit so that she could serve her sons a healthy and filling dinner.

Patricia says that she had never understood what it meant when she read that God would supply her needs; but when she opened that door, she understood completely. God had miraculously supplied her needs.

God always has another miracle. Claim it!

Lord, thank you for providing for us from your miraculous supply. Amen.

A Conception Miracle

Abbey had always wanted to have children. Her mother, sisters, aunts, and friends all had children; so why was she, at age thirty-five, having difficulty conceiving? She and her husband, Jeff, had been trying to conceive for two years with no success. They were referred to a fertility specialist, and after numerous tests, it was determined that Abbey suffered from premature ovarian failure. This diagnosis meant that her reproductive organs no longer functioned in such a way that she could conceive and carry a baby to birth. An expensive procedure involving an egg donor and in vitro fertilization was suggested as the only alternative to either surrogacy or adoption. None of these options interested Abbey and Jeff.

Abbey's disappointment and pain increased when, on the same day she received this devastating news, she went to the hospital to celebrate with a friend who had just given birth. She purposefully kept her visit brief and went home to drown in her sorrow. God sent some of her friends whom she viewed as earthly angels to pray with her and to encourage her; but she felt that because they had their own children, they could not possibly understand her pain.

Then Abbey met another woman who previously had been diagnosed with premature ovarian failure. This woman had not one but three children. Abbey realized that God is still performing miracles. So she threw away her ovulation kits and pregnancy tests and entered into prayer with her husband each morning. She remembered how God had blessed the barren Sarah, Hannah, Rachel, and Elizabeth. She came into a renewed understanding that God's promises are true, and she decided to stand on those promises. Seven months later, Abbey conceived; and in due time, Michala Gabrielle, named for the angels Michael and Gabriel, was born.

God always has another miracle. Claim it!

Lord, thank you for the miracle of birth. May we never treat it lightly or take it for granted. Amen.

A Fivefold Miracle

Michelle is an elementary school teacher. Although she was making a livable salary, she was not able to save any money. A parent of one of her students told her that it was easy to save. All she had to do was put a little aside from each paycheck, and she would be surprised to discover how fast it added up. Michelle decided to try it. Before long, she had saved $200 and was very proud of herself.

Then Michelle heard that the house of the same parent who had advised her to save money had burned to the ground. That family had lost everything. Michelle thought about the $200 and decided to give it to the family. After all, she would not have had the money had that parent not encouraged her to save. Against the advice of friends who told her just to give $50, Michelle took the entire amount and gave it to the family in need. It was amazing how good her gift made her feel. She knew she had done the right thing.

A few days later, Michelle got a letter from her father. He said that he was thinking about her and remembered what a hard time she had saving money and had decided to send her a little something to help. In the letter, he had enclosed a check for $1,000. It was a fivefold miracle!

God always has another miracle. Claim it!

Lord, help me be generous with my resources. I know that you will continue to bless me abundantly. Amen.

A Gift of Love

Four-year-old Angela was suffering from severe kidney failure and needed a kidney transplant immediately. After everyone in her family was tested, the closest match found was her grandmother, and the doctors did not recommend that transplant.

Not knowing what else to do, Angela's mother placed a personal ad in the local newspaper. She advertised for a kidney for her ailing daughter. She begged and prayed for someone to come forward to be tested. Although her family had little money and her husband had been out of work for some time, she offered to pay for the kidney that might save her daughter's life. She had no idea where she would get the money, but she knew that she would get it somehow.

A complete stranger responded to the ad. He was a better match for Angela than her grandmother, and he was younger and in better health. Without hesitation the man agreed to donate a kidney to Angela, and the major surgeries were arranged. He would not hear of accepting any payment for his kidney; he was just glad to be able to help a precious child of God.

Both surgeries were completed without complications. As soon as the donor was ambulatory, he went to check on Angela. He wanted to know how she was doing and if his gift had made a difference in her life. Angela's family was amazed that he was so concerned about their daughter and had made such a selfless gift of love.

Angela's mother had submitted the ad because she had run out of options. She dared to expect a miracle, and she got both a miracle and a gift of love.

God always has another miracle. Claim it!

Lord, I want to be selfless in my gift-giving to you and to others. Amen.

A Miracle of Friendship

A group of teenage friends living in Orlando, Florida, decided to go floating on boogie boards in Little Lake Conway one summer morning. These friends had floated together on the lake many times in the past, and they had no reason to believe that this time would be any different. What they did not know was that there were alligators in the lake.

Edna, fourteen years old, felt something grab her arm. She thought that one of her friends was playing with her until she realized she was being spun around and around. When she saw that an alligator had her in a death spin, she screamed and screamed while trying to pry the alligator's mouth open so that she could remove her arm. Most of her friends swam quickly to shore so that they could get help; but one friend, fourteen-year-old Amanda, refused to desert her friend Edna. By this time, Edna believed that she would surely die. She felt her arm snap as the alligator pulled her under the water, and she knew that she would drown and be eaten by the alligator. She thought that this was the way that God had intended for her to die.

Taking a different viewpoint, Amanda felt confident that God would save them both. She knew that she could not leave her friend. She never would have been able to live with her guilt if anything had happened to Edna. By working together, Amanda helped Edna free herself from the alligator. Discovering that Edna could not swim with her broken and badly damaged arm, Amanda managed to drag her to shore even though Edna was twice as big as Amanda.

The other friends on shore had gotten help, and Edna was rushed to the hospital where she received blood transfusions, was treated for a broken arm, and underwent surgery to clean debris from the muscles in her arm. Looking at Edna and Amanda, everyone wondered how Amanda had managed to save Edna. Amanda was willing to lay down her life for her friend, and God empowered her to save that friend. It was indeed a miracle of friendship.

God always has another miracle. Claim it!

Lord, give me the heart of a friend. I want you to use me to save others. Amen.

The Miracle of Redirection

On September 11, 2001, terrorists attacked our country. The attack came without warning, and many wondered where God was during the tragedy. God was right there with us. Had the terrorists attacked an hour later, there could have been 50,000 people in the World Trade Center. God miraculously redirected thousands so that the death toll was no higher than it was. In fact, only a tenth, a tithe, was claimed.

God redirected a businessman who was on a flight to New York on Monday evening, September 10, 2001. Just as his plane made plans to push away from the gate, the Spirit of God told him to get off the plane. The Spirit was so strong that he could not ignore it. He told the flight attendants that he had to get off the plane. Of course, they asked if he was ill. He told them that he was not and that though he could not explain it, he just had to get off the plane. He got off, and when the terrorists attacked, he was at home rather than in the midst of the chaos. God had miraculously redirected him.

Then there was the Australian Olympic swimmer who was on his way to the top of the World Trade Center when he realized that he had forgotten his camera. He went back to get it and missed the attack. God had also miraculously redirected him. Or perhaps you have heard the story of a woman who left the building to meet her father for breakfast. The plane hit just as she walked out of the building. Still again there was the father who took his son to school for his first day and was late for work. There were countless others who left the building to get a paper or a cup of coffee and many others who overslept and were late for work. So many more listened to the Spirit that told them to stay home from work that day. They were all miraculously redirected.

God redirects all of us daily. We must stay close to him to hear and know his voice. Sometimes there are warnings from deep within, but we ignore them. Start listening. God is speaking. Pray and meditate daily so that when the Spirit seeks to redirect you, you will hear and be obedient.

Yes, God was there during the attack. A tithe was sacrificed, but 90 percent were saved. It was a miracle.

God always has another miracle. Claim it!

Lord, I am listening for your voice. I want to be redirected by your Spirit. Breathe afresh on me. Amen.

PRAYERS

Therefore I tell you, whatever you ask for in prayer, believe that you have received it, and it will be yours.

—Mark 11:24

A Miracle Frequency

Byron Powell is an airline pilot, and he knows how important radios are to his occupation. Pilots have to be able to communicate with other aircraft and with air traffic controllers. Byron is especially pleased that his aircraft is equipped with the new digital radios because he is able to tune into more frequencies. All he has to do is turn the dials and knobs to select the right frequency, depress the mike button, and state his request. The other aircraft or air traffic controllers respond as appropriate.

But it was not the aircraft radio that concerned him as a van sped toward him and his copilot on the tarmac as they were making their way to their plane. There was no getting out of the way. Though the van missed the copilot, it hit Byron head on. He was knocked fifty feet into the air, and he bounced several times on the concrete ground. Even after he had finally landed firmly, his luggage was still spinning in the air. Byron was rushed to the hospital, and five hours later he miraculously walked out. He sustained a broken wrist but had suffered no greater injuries.

Byron recalls praying at the exact time the van hit him. He says that he was already on the right frequency for communicating with God. He keeps his dials and knobs on God's frequency, for he knows that he needs God every minute of his life. He did not have to waste time trying to tune in to God or introduce himself to a God with whom he had never been in contact. He was able to get right to the point and pray that God would hold his head in his hands and that he would not go under the van. Miraculously, although Byron hit the ground several times, his head never hit and he did not go under the van.

Bryon believes that God was in the control tower responding to his Mayday distress call. He is so glad that he was tuned to God's frequency. What about you?

God always has another miracle. Claim it!

Lord, help me stay tuned to your frequency every minute of my day and night. Amen.

Prayer Conditioned

I received a letter from a grandmother who wanted to share her grandbaby's miracle story with me. The baby, Briana, was born on Palm Sunday with heart complications. After staying in the neonatal intensive care unit for four days, she underwent heart surgery. Four days later, she had a second heart surgery. Just think: a new baby had two heart surgeries and survived! On the thirteenth day of her life, Briana was discharged from the hospital. It was a miracle!

But the miracles were not confined to Briana's survival of the heart surgeries. While she was in intensive care during the first four days of her life, the family pastor went to see her. He announced to Briana that her pastor and her grandmother had come to pray for her. Although Briana had been crying before the pastor's visit, upon hearing his voice she immediately stopped crying, wrapped her fingers around the pastor's finger, closed her eyes, and seemed to be aware of the prayer for her recovery.

The pastor and the grandmother returned to visit Briana before her second surgery. Again she was crying, and again, when prayer was announced, she wrapped her fingers around the pastor's finger, closed her eyes, and assumed an attitude of prayer. There must have been something calming about the pastor's manner that assured Briana that help was on the way. In the pastor's words, "Briana was prayer conditioned."

How wonderful it is to be raised in an atmosphere of prayer. How wonderful to know that prayer changes things. How blessed we all are to have pastors who bring peace and calm to our lives. How blessed we are to have children who are prayer conditioned. Briana experienced the miracle of medical technology and the miracle of prayer.

God always has another miracle. Claim it!

Lord, help us all become prayer conditioned. Amen.

The Miracle Vote

Cascade United Methodist Church in Atlanta, Georgia, outgrew its five-and-a-half million-dollar edifice in less than nine years. There were not enough parking spaces, not enough classrooms to accommodate the more than fifty weekly Bible study classes, not enough seats in the sanctuary, and not enough offices for the ministerial and program staff. Cascade sought to relieve this situation by moving to three Sunday morning worship services. To everyone's surprise, even though the time of the first service was 7:00 A.M., worshipers came to that service in large numbers. The neighboring company's parking lot was used to provide additional parking, and a shuttle service was activated. Some Bible study classes were held in homes, and lounges were converted into office space.

But Cascade needed more. A development committee was organized, and the church purchased over one hundred acres of land in a nearby community. Cascade felt certain that this land would provide all that would be needed for the next century. However, there was a problem. The property was zoned for business use and would have to be rezoned if a church was to be built. This did not initially seem like a huge problem, as the property had originally been a farm. Yet, there were members of the city council who felt that the city would not be able to collect the much-needed taxes if a church was built on the property. Cascade proposed a compromise with the city, promising to build some houses on the property so that part of the land could be taxed.

The time of the city council's vote approached, and the members of Cascade united in prayer, praying that the zoning would be changed. One of the church's members was a city councilman; however, he was excused from having to vote because of his assumed bias. There was only one literal vote taken, which was four-to-three in favor of changing the zoning so that a church could be built. But as far as the members of Cascade were concerned, the council's vote was secondary to "God's vote," which was one-to-nothing in their favor!

The members of Cascade had prayed for a miracle, and they had gotten one. Now they are ready to proceed with building for Christian ministry into the twenty-first century.

God always has another miracle. Claim it!

Lord, we know that when you are for us, it does not matter who is against us. Amen.

Safe Delivery

Marion is an inmate in a women's state prison. She never thought that she would be an inmate, and she really never imagined that she would be pregnant when she entered prison. She had always dreamed of enjoying her pregnancy at home and going to a hospital to deliver her baby. She dreamed that, after an uncomplicated delivery, she would joyously take her baby home. Reality was nothing like her dreams.

When Marion entered prison, she was past her pregnancy due date. After she had been in prison a week, the doctors decided to induce labor. During the procedure, the doctors discovered that there was no heartbeat and that the baby had been without the amniotic fluid that usually surrounds the unborn child. The next decision was to perform a caesarean section and remove what they believed to be a dead child.

Marion could not believe what was happening. Not only was she delivering her baby as a prison inmate, but also she was thought to be delivering a dead child. Marion began to pray silently. She concentrated on communing with God. She listened for his voice. She waited for an answer or a sense of direction. She needed a word, a sound, a feeling—something.

After what seemed like an eternity, she felt a calm spirit surround her, and she heard a voice that said, "It's OK." Then she felt the baby kick, and the heart monitor showed activity. Although the doctors were afraid that the baby would have numerous infections as a result of being outside the amniotic fluid, a healthy baby was delivered. It was a miracle.

God always has another miracle. Claim it!

Lord, thank you for safe "deliveries" of all kinds, even in difficult and unusual surroundings. Amen.

The Miraculous Name of Jesus

Sixteen years ago, my husband was diagnosed with a condition called diverticulitis. In its most dangerous state, bleeding of the colon occurs. If the bleeding cannot be stopped, part or even all of the colon must be removed. Those diagnosed with this condition must be careful to avoid nuts and seeds, medicines containing aspirin, and stress.

Of course, as a pastor, my husband was often subject to stress, but he had done fairly well avoiding the other dangerous conditions—that is, until this year. When the bleeding started, he had to be admitted to the hospital and then was given nine units of blood. (During a previous hospitalization this year, he had received two units of blood.) He was resting and praying that the bleeding would stop so that he would not require surgery. He kept reflecting on the many times he had told others that the power to heal them was within. All they had to do was call on the name of Jesus. Then he started calling on the name of Jesus, believing that he would not need surgery.

At the same time that this revelation came to him, I was on the phone with a woman in our church who is a prayer warrior. She served as a pastor for eighteen years and continues to minister to others in a nonpastoral role. She asked me what my husband's medical condition was. Once I had explained the condition to her, she said, "Let's pray." She began by binding up everything that was harmful in the name of Jesus, and she prayed for healing in the name of Jesus.

By the time I got to my husband's hospital room the next day, he told me that he would not need surgery. He had prayed and had felt the prayers in which I participated. He claimed his healing in the name of Jesus, and it was so. He was released from the hospital the next day. There is miraculous power in that name.

God always has another miracle. Claim it!

Holy Father, help us remember to pray, believing in the precious name of Jesus. Amen.

The E-mail Miracle

I receive many e-mails that request the receiver to pass them on. Most of the time, I just delete them. But one e-mail that I received just before hurricane Ivan touched down in the United States got my attention. You may remember that the hurricane was headed for Mobile. Well, some of the people in Mobile started an e-mail requesting prayer. It stated that Jesus was able to speak peace to the winds and the waves and that he is still able to quiet storms. Each recipient was asked to join with the people of Mobile in prayer and to pass the e-mail on.

I stopped what I was doing and started praying that the storm would quiet and that Mobile would be spared. I even spoke to some family members in Mobile who said that they had prayed and had decided not to evacuate. They had spoken with some friends who did evacuate and discovered that it had taken them more than seven hours to drive from Mobile to Montgomery—two to three times more than the normal driving time.

Jesus told us that if we have faith the size of a mustard seed, we can move mountains. I kept remembering mustard seed faith as I joined in prayer with those who had sent the e-mail. Those miracle prayers must have moved Ivan, because the hurricane spared Mobile severe damage and was even reduced to a tropical storm.

I heard a reporter say that Mobile was lucky. I knew he was wrong. The people of Mobile had prayed, and they were blessed by a miracle.

God always has another miracle. Claim it!

Lord, give us the mustard seed faith that moves hurricanes. Amen.

A Miraculous Birth

The Clark family was traveling by car when they were involved in a head-on collision. Mrs. Clark was ten weeks pregnant, and she arrived at the hospital in a coma. Mr. Clark was dead on arrival. Relatives were contacted, and the decision was made to try to save Mrs. Clark and her baby even if she remained in the coma.

Family visited regularly and talked to the comatose expectant mother. The hospital staff did all they could to monitor the baby's progress. No one knew whether the mother or the baby would make it until the baby could survive on its own. Everyone prayed for a miracle.

The doctors informed the family that it would not be advisable to attempt to deliver the baby before a thirty-four-week gestation period. This meant that the mother and the baby had to survive twenty-four weeks. The family prayed as the waiting began.

Twenty-four weeks later, a five-pound-twelve-ounce baby boy was delivered by caesarean section. He was named Michael, and his birth was nothing short of a miracle.

Michael's aunt and uncle are raising him along with their

own daughter, who is just a few months older than Michael. They feel as though they have twins, but they are still praying that someday Michael's mother will wake up and care for him.

Michael's grandparents consider Michael to be the light of their lives. He has given them hope for the future. He is their shining star, their miracle. They pray for another miracle—that their daughter will awaken. Let us all join them in that prayer.

God always has another miracle. Claim it!

Lord, thank you for the miraculous birth of Michael. Bless his aunt and uncle, his grandparents, and the cousin he may come to know as a twin sister. Keep his mother in the cradle of your loving arms. Amen.

A Double Miracle

Rudi was in Russia visiting a printing plant where Bibles are printed. Rudi knew that few Bibles had been available in that part of the world, so he decided to purchase all the Bibles that had just been printed and send them to Siberia, where some of his friends were starting new churches. The total cost was much more money than he had, but he had felt the urge to send those much-needed Bibles anyway. Somehow he just knew that those Bibles could and would be used. He also knew that God would provide a miracle to pay for them.

Rudi sent the Bibles, along with a note stating how he had

decided to purchase them on the spur of the moment. Some time later his friends in Siberia told him that there had been no Bibles where they had been starting the new churches.

As Russians were converted to Christianity, they wanted to study the Word. These new Christians were told to pray that God would supply them with his Word. They prayed fervently for a week, and at the end of that week, the Bibles arrived. Needless to say, they were overjoyed to see how quickly and specifically God answers prayers.

Rudi knew that it had been the Holy Spirit who had prompted him to purchase and send the Bibles, making him a participant in the miracle the Russians had prayed for. Just as miraculously, many friends provided the money needed to cover the cost of the Bibles. It was a double miracle!

God always has another miracle. Claim it!

Lord, as you supply our need for your Word, teach us to read it, learn it, and live it every day. Amen.

Intercessory Prayer

Andy was diagnosed with an aggressive brain tumor. The doctors said that surgery, radiation, and chemotherapy offered little hope, and they estimated he could survive no more than a few months. Nevertheless, against all odds, Andy decided to go ahead with surgery. Following surgery, he endured both radiation and painful chemotherapy.

But that was not all Andy decided to do. He asked his church members to pray for him. He and his wife met regularly with the saints of the church who laid hands on him and prayed for his healing. His wife boldly announced to God, "I know you can do it!" She expected a miracle.

Today Andy is cancer free. The brain tumor, as well as the growths that appeared near his heart and were never surgically removed, are gone. The medical community cannot explain what happened, but the religious community knows that God performed a miracle.

Hundreds of scientific studies show that religious people are healthier. The neurooncologist who treated Andy's cancer said that faith cannot be ignored. There just seems to be some ingredient in therapy that is associated with faith.

Andy, his wife, and his church family know that prayer is the ingredient that leads to miracles of healing. They know that God always has another miracle. They claimed it!

Holy Father, thank you for the healing power of prayer. Amen.

Agreeing in Prayer

Jim was diagnosed with terminal lung cancer. His doctor told him that he had only a few months to live. Of course, surgery might prolong his life by a few more months, but death was certain within the year. Jim thought about his four-year-old daughter and accepted the fact that he would never see her grow up, attend college, get married, and have children. He resigned himself to death. He did not even want the surgery that his wife, Maggie, begged him to proceed with.

Maggie could not accept his decision. She knew that she would have to find someone to agree with her in prayer that Jim would not die. She desperately wanted him to live to see their four-year-old daughter as an adult. Just thinking about their daughter gave her an idea. She called the child to her and asked if she believed that her daddy would not die. The child said that she knew her daddy would not die. Maggie was so encouraged by her child's positive response that she asked her to pray with her. She held her child, and together they prayed, agreeing that Jim would live long past the time the doctors had predicted. All the while they were praying, Maggie remembered the scripture, "If two of you on earth agree about anything you ask for, it will be done for you by my Father in heaven" (Matthew 18:19).

Jim finally agreed to have the surgery, and he lived to see their child reach adulthood. It was a miracle. Maggie knew that the scripture she had believed had required only that two agree. It did not require that they both be adults!

God always has another miracle. Claim it!

Lord, give us that childlike faith that expects and receives miracles. Amen.

Answered Prayer

The downturn in the economy had been particularly hard for one family, and as Christmas approached, they were not sure how they would make ends meet. Both the father and the mother had lost their jobs due to downsizing, the baby was sick and needed expensive medicine, and the rental house in which they lived had been sold. On top of all that, they had to move. All the family could do was pray, and pray they did.

There is something unusual about sincere and fervent prayer. It inspires those praying to get up off their knees and hustle. So, after the prayer, the father and mother started talking about the various courses of action open to them. They thought about trying to become apartment managers so that they would have a place to live with free or reduced rent. They also talked about asking the owner of the grocery store where they shopped to extend their credit until they had some income. But they had no solution for the expensive medicine their baby needed.

While they were reviewing their situation, they received a phone call from a friend who told them of an apartment building that desperately needed a manager. They immediately made an appointment to meet the owner, and they were hired. They explained their cash flow situation, and the property owner said that he also owned a store in which the father could work extra hours. The family was overjoyed and grateful to God, but they still needed the baby's medicine. So the father explained the baby's needs and asked for a cash advance. To his great surprise, he discovered that the owner's store was a pharmacy. The owner said that he would be happy to run a tab for them so that they could get the medicine they needed. It was a miracle.

God always has another miracle. Claim it!

Lord, you are always working to provide for your children. Make us your agents, helping those in need and witnessing to your love. Amen.

The Miracle of Praying for Direction

John had been suffering from a painful nose and ear condition. His breathing was labored and his hearing was diminished. He had been to see several doctors, and they all told him that he would need immediate surgery. Somehow John was not willing to accept the doctors' recommendation. He had a very busy teaching schedule, and he was not sure when he would have time for the surgery. He decided to think about it.

While teaching one of his classes, the pain struck him severely. Then John decided to do what he should have done in the first place. He prayed for direction. He asked God to show him how he could fit the surgery into his schedule.

A few days later, John felt a tingling sensation move across his face and ear. He noticed immediately that he no longer felt pain. His breathing and hearing had returned to normal. He checked with his doctors, and they confirmed that, miraculously, he had been healed.

John remembered that God answers before we call and is able to do far more than we ask or imagine. I wonder how often we, like John, make decisions to think about the situations that we face. How long does it take us to realize that we can do nothing by ourselves? We have no power. We need God's direction. We must remember what a mighty God we serve!

John now knows that God always has another miracle. He just had to claim it!

Lord, thank you for the miracles that are ours for the asking. Amen.

ESCAPES

Even though I walk
through the valley of the shadow of death,
I will fear no evil,
for you are with me;
your rod and your staff,
they comfort me.

—Psalm 23:4

A Watery Escape

Melissa did not know how she escaped her SUV once it had gone off the bridge into the river. All she knew was that she had hit the metal grating of the bridge, her air bag had opened, and she had fallen off the bridge inside her vehicle.

Melissa had been talking to her sister on her hands-free cell phone at about one o'clock in the afternoon when her car skidded toward the guardrail. She is not sure what caused the skid. It could have been the wind or the heavy rain; nevertheless, as she felt the car start to skid, she may have overcorrected. As her car plunged into the water, she thought that she was going to die. Her sister heard her screams and knew something was wrong but could not do anything about it.

Miraculously, Melissa did not lose consciousness and managed to unfasten her seat belt and float through a broken window. She started kicking and praying that she would reach the surface one way or another. Somehow she felt that she was not

61

supposed to die like this. When she reached the surface, she was too tired to breathe. She just floated and rested on the surface of the water. Then she heard cheers. People on the bridge had watched the crash and were elated that she had survived. A diver from the county sheriff's office rescued her, and she was taken to the hospital. She had no major injuries—only minor cuts and bruises. It was a miracle.

Melissa kept saying, "I don't know how I got out." Well, Melissa, I do know. It was a miracle.

God always has another miracle. Claim it!

Lord, you are busy saving us every day. Thank you. Amen.

A Miraculous Rescue

All of a sudden, Sara realized that she was lost in the snow-covered mountains. After trying to signal for help, she decided to use the survival techniques she had learned in the fifth grade. She collected whatever liquid that she had with her and that she could gather from the elements. She built a snow cave for warmth, and she settled down to wait for her rescue.

She waited for three days, and then she decided that it was time to prepare for her impending death. She gathered what she had with her and found that she could use what she had to write notes to her loved ones. She wrote a note to her fiancée with her eyeliner pencil. She told him that she loved him and that she would always be his guardian angel.

She wished that she had brought a cell phone with her so that she could have attempted to make a call. She had thought that the phone would not work in the mountains.

After writing her notes, she thought about the date. It was March 6, the anniversary of the deaths of her mother and grandmother. She began to believe that it was a fitting date for her death, but she did not want to die. As the cold began to overtake her and as she felt hunger pangs engulf her, she prayed for a miracle. Somehow, someway, someone would have to find her. Only God could make that happen.

Just about the time Sara had given up, John Amos, who was riding with a group on snowmobiles, found her. Sara could not believe her eyes. How had they happened to come along? It must have been a miracle.

God always has another miracle. Claim it!

Lord, I know you are in the miracle business. Let me never give up hope. Amen.

Blessed Friendship

Eighty-one-year-old Jack lives in a senior citizens' high-rise apartment complex in New Orleans. He has a dog and not much else, but the dog is a great companion. Jack was told to vacate his apartment because hurricane Katrina was on its way. A shelter was being provided for the residents of his apartment complex.

Jack got his dog and made his way to the shelter. When he got there, he was told that he could stay, but dogs were not allowed. Jack was not about to leave his dog, so he turned around and headed home.

When he got back home, the apartment complex was locked. He wondered how he would get in. He walked around the building and found a window that had blown out during the beginning stages of the storm. He managed to reach that window. He threw his dog in first, and then he climbed in. He and his dog made their way to his apartment and snuggled together to ride out the storm that was growing more severe.

Jack did not know what was happening. The winds and the rain were overwhelming, but he managed to stay dry and unhurt. There was no electricity and very little food, but he and his dog shared what little there was. Somehow his building complex and his apartment survived the onslaught. After three days, he noticed activity outside the building, and he and his dog were rescued.

Many asked Jack why he had stayed behind. He simply said that he could not leave his best friend. The entire time that he was talking about the storm they had survived together, the dog was showering kisses all over Jack's face. Even the dog was grateful for their miraculous blessing.

God always has another miracle. Claim it!

Lord, thank you for our four-legged friends who demonstrate your unconditional love. Amen.

Miraculous Protection

His name is Murtza Ali, and he was eight months old when he and his mother were involved in a devastating earthquake that occurred in India in January 2001. Murtza and his mother lived in Bhuj. I can just imagine that he and his mother were sharing loving moments just before the quake struck. They had gone to Bhuj's Kansara Market. She was holding him when the building collapsed.

The moments that followed the quake must have been filled with confusion. I am sure survivors were wondering what had happened. Being from California, I am very familiar with the aftereffects of an earthquake. You feel and sometimes even see the earth open up. Cracks suddenly appear on the walls, and dishes crash to the floor. There is nowhere to go. Everything is shaking and moving. All you can do is pray.

Murtza and his mother were buried in the rubble for three days. When they were discovered, he was still sitting on her lap. She was dead, and he was covered in her blood; but her body had shielded him. The warmth of her body had served to insulate him and keep him warm. I can imagine that as she felt the building collapse, she managed to shift Murtza to her lap in an effort to protect him. She succeeded.

A Border Security Forces assistant commandant discovered the mother and child and saw some movement from the baby. He took the baby in his hands and found that it was alive. It was a miracle. The baby had survived for three days.

Murtza was rushed to a medical center, and family members

were located. Just a few hours later, little Murtza was conscious and smiling. His mother had saved his life. Tens of thousands of people died, but little Murtza lived!

That mother demonstrated her love with her body. I am not sure she knew what was happening or what she was doing, but her instincts told her to try to protect her child. She did that, and God used her as a beautiful illustration of a love that shielded until a miraculous rescue could occur. May she rest in peace as one who gave her life for her child.

God always has another miracle. Claim it!

Lord, give us an unselfish spirit that demonstrates our love for one another. Amen.

The Cell Phone Miracle

When John Stockton left his teaching job for a brief vacation in the beautiful waters near Hawaii, he had no idea that he might lose his life. He set out in his kayak expecting a smooth sail and a glorious experience as he enjoyed the water and all of God's creation. But a storm arose, and he could not get back to shore. By the third day in the water, the storm had knocked him out of the kayak repeatedly. He paddled for twenty-two hours trying to get to shore. When he was too exhausted to paddle any longer, he set his alarm clock to awaken him so that he could start to paddle again. Although his hands were blistered and he was terribly sunburned, he kept hoping that someone would discover him.

Meanwhile, Jack's mother was informed that her son was missing, and she boarded a plane to Hawaii in hopes of being near when he was found. She knew about the storm, and she knew that the likelihood of his survival was slim.

When John was thirty miles from shore, he remembered his cell phone. He thought that it was very unlikely that he would get a signal, but he tried anyway. Miraculously, he was successful. He asked the emergency service to send a search party. A little while later, a plane flew overhead, but it did not see him. He called again and told them to come out farther. Then his phone ceased to work. The battery was dead.

By the fifth day in the water, John had drifted eighty-six miles out to sea. Seeing no sign of rescue, he prepared to die. Before long, he was spotted and rescued.

His mother, still en route to Hawaii, was handed a note informing her that her son had been found alive and had been taken to the hospital. She knew it was a miracle.

God always has another miracle. Claim it!

Lord, no matter how far we drift, you can still save us. Amen.

Miraculous Kisses

George Mitchell is eighty years old, and his dog, Frisky, is nineteen years old—or, in dog years, about 133. Several years ago, Frisky appeared on George's doorstep, and George's wife told him to let Frisky in because the dog had adopted him. Although George's wife died a few years after Frisky came to live with them, George is convinced that she set his miracle in motion the day she told him to welcome Frisky in.

Frisky gave George a reason to live when hurricane Katrina slammed the Biloxi home in which they lived. Their home was flooded, and George and Frisky were treading water and swimming, just trying to survive. After about four hours, George decided to give up. He was just too tired to continue. He had found a spot on his floating mattress, and he closed his eyes, hoping to see his wife again. But Frisky would not let him give up. Frisky just kept licking and kissing George until he was fully conscious and continued to tread, keeping them both alive.

After what seemed like a lifetime, the water receded enough for George and Frisky to make it out of the house and get to a place where help was waiting. They were taken to a hospital and, at George's insistence, placed in bed together.

George says that Frisky is the reason he is still living. He knows how old the dog is, and he believes that the dog is waiting to cross the Jordan River with him. He knows that they both nearly crossed the Jordan during the hurricane. Perhaps it was wondering what would happen to Frisky, along with those miraculous kisses, that kept George treading.

God always has another miracle. Claim it!

Lord, you even send dog kisses to save us. Thank you. Amen.

A Miraculous Survival

Donna knew that she was about to be crushed to death by the tractor-trailer that was headed toward her car. As the eighteen-wheeler struck her car, she asked for forgiveness of her sins and hoped that she was headed to heaven. It was a miracle that she did not die right away. Her car was flattened, and she knew that emergency workers were trying to pry her from the wreckage. Her body seemed to be wedged toward the roof of her car, and her head was bleeding.

Realizing that she was still alive, Donna started reciting the Twenty-third Psalm. One of the emergency workers held her hand, and a nurse called her husband. Inflatable lifts were placed under the trailer to secure it, but it still shifted, clamping further down on Donna's head. After more than two hours, a hydraulic lift was used to raise the trailer, and Donna was able to crawl out. She was rushed to the hospital, and doctors were amazed to discover that she had only minor injuries. It was a miracle.

When Donna's husband saw what was left of her car, he knew that if she had been any taller, she probably would not have survived. Being just over five feet tall, she was able to fit in the small space left between her car and the trailer.

Although Donna knew that the emergency workers were not being paid to hold her hand and comfort her, she was grateful for their kindness. Her prayers, her size, the scriptures, and the workers were all a part of her miracle.

God always has another miracle. Claim it!

Lord, so many elements go into the everyday miracles we experience. Thank you. Amen.

An Unusual Landing

My unofficially adopted son, Brian, developed a love of flying. He decided to take flying lessons, learned to fly, and obtained his pilot's license. He told me that there was no feeling in the world like flying and that he truly loved it. Recently he flew a passenger from Atlanta to Cleveland, Ohio. The flight was smooth; they transacted their business and started the return flight. Although Brian had intended to stop in Knoxville, Tennessee, to refuel, his fuel level indicated that there were thirty minutes of flying time remaining; and he was only ten minutes from his destination. He decided not to stop. Four minutes later his fuel indicator registered empty. He was in the air and out of fuel. Knowing that he had to land the plane as quickly as possible, he looked for a clearing. Spotting one, he headed toward it. He did not see the power lines in which his plane became ensnared. The plane hit the power lines with a tremendous bang and became twisted in them and held upside down. Brian expected the plane to crash to the ground, but the power lines held it securely.

No longer expecting the plane to crash, Brian and his passenger decided to unfasten their seat belts and right themselves up. Brian ended up right in front of the door. He thought the door would open and he would fall to the ground, but the door remained shut. Believing the door to be jammed, Brian had lots of time to consider his predicament.

He had not seen the power lines, and yet they had kept him from crashing to the ground. This was his first miraculous blessing. Then, once having hit the power lines, they had not electrocuted either him or his passenger. Neither had the lines automatically resurged. Normally power lines attempt three times to resurge. Any resurgence would have killed both of them. This was his second miraculous blessing.

Six hours later, Brian and his passenger were rescued by fire-fighters. When the fireman attempted to open the door against which Brian was leaning, it popped open with ease. The door was not jammed. The fact that it had not opened when he had leaned against it was his third miraculous blessing.

Both Brian and his passenger were thoroughly cold and exhausted, but they were alive and unhurt. This was the fourth miraculous blessing!

Brian called me when he got home and told me how grateful he is to God for these miraculous blessings. I told him seriously to consider his life and mission, for surely God has some great work for him—and for all of us—to do.

God always has another miracle. Claim it!

Lord, thank you for being the pilot of our lives. We are always safe when we allow you to fly. Amen.

A Sixteen-Hour Survival

Sarah and Emily, former collegiate rowers, were competing in the Atlanta Rowing Race when a wave flipped their rowboat in choppy seas. At the time the rowboat flipped, they were in their cabin; but they managed to swim out of it. They discovered that their lifeboat had floated away, so they crawled on top of their overturned boat and hung on.

The two women knew that their only chance of survival was to cling to the hull of their capsized boat, so that is what they did. They had no idea that they would have to hold on for sixteen hours. They were attempting to row 2,913 nautical miles, more than 3,300 land miles, from the Canary Islands to Antigua in the Caribbean.

They managed to send an emergency beacon that alerted the Coast Guard via satellite. The Coast Guard found them and sent a ship to pick them up. They were 1,300 miles east of Puerto Rico and were in surprisingly good condition.

The fact that they were able to get out of their cabin after the ten- to twelve-foot wave washed over their boat and flipped it, the fact that they were able to crawl on top of their boat and send an emergency beacon, and the fact that they were able to hang on for sixteen hours all witness to the miraculous saving power of God.

God always has another miracle. Claim it!

Lord, thank you for saving us when our ambitious desire to do spectacular things endangers our lives. Amen.

The Miracle of Life

If you are reading this story, then you have experienced the miracle of life for one more year. At the beginning of each new year, I am reminded that not everyone who was alive this time last year is alive now. The following story is an illustration of that very fact. As you read it, remember to thank God that you are still experiencing the miracle of life.

A few years ago, a five-year-old girl, Ruby, and her mother were in an automobile accident and crashed 150 feet down a ravine. The mother was severely injured, but Ruby was not hurt. Ruby tried to wake her mother up so that they could get help, but her mother did not respond. Ruby just stayed with her mother and waited for someone to discover them.

After a few days, Ruby's mother died. Ruby was hungry, and God directed her to the dry noodles and Gatorade that were in the car. Ruby ate and slept and tried to awaken her mother. She did not know her mother was dead, and she did not know how to ask for help. All she could do through the days and nights that followed was wait.

Ten days later state Department of Transportation workers discovered the wreckage while repairing a road barrier. They wondered how the little girl had survived sitting next to the badly decomposing body of her mother.

We will never know why the wreckage was not discovered sooner or why the daughter survived; but we do know that God was with that child and that she was granted the miracle of life for at least one more year.

God always has another miracle. Claim it!

Gracious God, thank you for another year of the miracle of life. Amen.

The Breath of God

Two young men were having a delightful conversation while walking down the street on a beautiful, clear afternoon. There was no wind, and the sky was bright and clear. As the afternoon progressed, it even got hot. But the two young men were so happy to be enjoying the sun that they continued their walk.

They noticed a mother and her young daughter walking out of a card shop. The mother was reading a recently purchased card to her daughter. The mother was so engrossed in the card that she did not notice the bus that was rapidly approaching. Within seconds the bus would hit the couple. One of the men tried to yell a warning, but nothing came out of his mouth. Just then a breeze blew the card out of the mother's hand. As she turned to grab it, she fell, knocking both herself and her child out of the path of the bus, which whizzed by. She did not even realize that both she and her daughter were almost hit.

The young men wondered where that burst of wind had come from. How had it been strong enough to blow the card out of the mother's hand? There had not even been the slightest hint of wind seconds earlier. Why hadn't either of them been able to shout to the mother, warning her of the impending danger? Then they reflected that if they had cried out, the mother might have looked up but failed to move out of the path of the bus. They further reflected that the passing bus had not created the wind because the wind had come from the opposite direction. The only explanation is that the wind was the miraculous breath of God, blowing to protect both mother and child.

God always has another miracle. Claim it!

Lord, I wonder how often your miracles blow by us unnoticed. Remind us to look up and give thanks. Amen.

A Miraculous Emergency Call

Did you know that dogs can be trained to dial 911? If ever there was a miracle story, this is one!

Leana has a four-year-old Rottweiler named Faith. She helped train Faith at an Assistance Dog Club. Leana is wheelchair bound and suffers from grand mal seizures. Faith is very much attuned to Leana's condition and uses her nose to detect changes in Leana's body chemistry—a scientifically proven capability of dogs.

Faith seemed to know that something was up the day that Leana fell out of her wheelchair. Throughout the day, Faith had been clinging to and touching Leana. Faith sensed a change in Leana's body chemistry and tried to stay close. When the fall occurred, Faith knew to knock the phone's receiver off the hook, use her nose to push the 911 button on speed dial, and bark convincingly.

The 911 dispatcher could tell from the tenor and persistence of the barking, which was directed into the receiver, that the dog was definitely trying to tell him something. He took that something to be that immediate help was needed. So he dispatched the emergency workers. Faith not only knew how to dial 911, but she also knew how to unlock the door and let the emergency workers in.

Leana had not actually suffered a seizure, but her liver was not properly processing her seizure medication, which is what had prompted the fall. Leana had to stay in the hospital three weeks. She knows that her dog miraculously saved her life.

God always has another miracle. Claim it!

Lord, thank you for creating animals who not only are our friends, but also help save our lives. Amen.

Surviving Against the Odds

In a portable toilet in a park, a newborn baby boy was deposited. The temperature was twenty degrees, the toilet was filled with water, and the newborn was dressed in clothes made for a stuffed animal. Yet, he survived.

His teenage father had left him in the toilet and had thought that he would die before being discovered, but God had other plans. God sent one of his children to the park; the man passed by the toilet and heard the cries of the newborn. God was at his miracle-working best.

Why did this young father choose to deposit his son in such a manner? The baby's teenage mother suggested that the baby be left at the church or a hospital. She knew about the safe haven laws that allow parents who do not want their newborns to leave them at hospitals or police or fire stations within seventy-two hours of birth. No questions are asked. The baby is checked and then sent to a foster home. What was this young father thinking?

The mother had concealed her pregnancy from her friends and family. She delivered her son alone in the tub in the family bathroom. She cleaned the baby up, dressed him in some clothes that fit her teddy bear, and called the baby's father. She told him about the safe haven laws and explained that no questions would be asked, but the father decided to take the baby to the park.

Since the discovery of the newborn, the father has been arrested and charged with first-degree intentional homicide. It is only by the grace of God that the baby survived. It was a miracle.

God always has another miracle. Claim it!

Lord, help us teach our young people the consequences of sex and the value of human life. Thank you for saving the lives we would so carelessly throw away. Amen.

The Immediate Response

It was a beautiful spring day, and I had just taken my mother back to her assisted living facility after we had had lunch together. I was approaching my exit on the expressway when I noticed a tire in the middle of my driving lane. I swerved to avoid hitting the tire and tried to return to the right-hand lane, but I lost control of the car. I knew that I was headed for a crash and prayed that I would not get hurt. The car headed off the expressway down an embankment, hit the dirt wall, spun around, flipped over, and stopped. Once the car stopped, I realized that I was OK; but the car was lying on the driver's side, and I wondered how I would be able to get out. I prayed, "Lord, how am I going to get out of this car?" As soon as the prayer was uttered, the car righted itself, and I opened the door. What a miraculous and immediate response that was!

Several people stopped to help me. One man ran to the car as he called 911 on his cell phone. He begged me not to try to get out of the car. When I convinced him that I was all right, he asked me just to sit for a few minutes. I sat there, looked for my earrings that had come off during the crash, put them back on, and reflected on how good God had been to me.

When the sheriff and the fire department paramedics arrived, they asked if the driver had already gone to the hospital. I told them that I was the driver. The paramedics asked me if I knew where I was and what day it was. Satisfied with my answers, they cancelled the ambulance. I called my husband to come to get me. He asked if I was all right and told me that he was on his way. When he saw the car, he just shook his head and thanked God that I had survived.

After calling for the police to come and have the car towed, the sheriff prepared to leave. He said, "Ma'am, I won't tell you to have a blessed day, because you already have."

God always has another miracle. Claim it!

Lord, thank you for being with me every step of the way. Thank you for responses that are immediate and miraculous. Amen.

HEALINGS

I will heal my people and will let them enjoy abundant peace and security.

—Jeremiah 33:6b

Natural Healing

Acquired Immune Deficiency Syndrome (AIDS) affects millions of people around the world. There are more than 900,000 persons in the United States living with the disease. However, there is hope, and the death rate of affected people is decreasing. Consider Niro Markoff, who was diagnosed with AIDS-Related Complex (ARC) more than twenty years ago. Her symptoms included thrush (a fungal disease marked by white patches in the mouth), diarrhea, exhaustion, and night sweats. She was given eighteen months to live.

Niro did not believe the doctors. She knew that they did not have the power to put a time limit on her life. She knew that God alone had that power, so she began to make radical changes in her style of living. She created a therapy program called Self Healing AIDS Related Experiment (SHARE). This program consisted of meditation, visualization, exercise, and the exclusive consumption of natural foods. Through meditation, she became closer to God and concentrated on his will for her life. She believed that God willed her to live, not die. She learned to visualize the AIDS-Related Complex leaving her body. She knew that there were toxins associated with ARC, and all she needed to do was flush those toxins out.

Although the exercise and natural foods helped do that, she needed to see it happening. Meditation taught her that she had to visualize the toxins leaving her body before she could realize their having gone. After ten months, all traces of illness had vanished.

What happened? Did her SHARE therapy program effect a miracle? What component of the program was the most effective? Was it the meditation, and could meditation alone work? Was it the visualization or the exercise? Could it have been the natural foods? Or was God rewarding her faithfulness? Although we may never know, Niro has not abandoned the therapy program and still practices it daily.

Niro says that there is a divine order, and it has been her guide. She is currently teaching others to use her program. Although she wants her students to learn to tap into their own healing powers, she knows that God is in control. By God's power, she has not had any trace of HIV for over twenty years. It is a miracle.

God always has another miracle. Claim it!

Lord, we are so quick to give up when adversity strikes, but you are in control. Give us the faith that will lead us to the natural healing only you can give. Amen.

Bionic Arms

Can you imagine not having arms? How would you wash your body, eat your food, comb your hair, or brush your teeth?

Even more important, how would you hug and hold your loved ones? It is hard to imagine, isn't it? Well, for an eleven-year-old girl, having no arms was not her imagination; it was reality. Her name is Diamond Excell, and she was born without arms.

I know that when we are expecting a birth in our families, our primary prayer is that the baby will be normal. That means that we want the baby to have the right number of fingers and toes, and, of course, we expect the baby to have arms. But Diamond's mother welcomed a baby without arms. She named her Diamond, for she was rare indeed.

Diamond's rarity became evident as she grew up. She learned to wash her body, eat her food, comb her hair, brush her teeth, and even write with her feet. But she could not hug her mother until she experienced the miracle of bionic arms.

An inventor teamed up with a prosthetist to make motorized arms for Diamond. The arms' motors open and close three joints and are activated by signals that the brain generates when a muscle is flexed. The team modeled hands for Diamond after those of one of her cousins. Diamond was then challenged to master the use of the bionic arms. She was confident, however, that mastering their use would be easy. She demonstrated by picking up a bag by its handle using a finger and a thumb.

Never having been able to hug anyone, Diamond anxiously put those miracle arms around her mother. Her mother said that words could not express the way she felt when she was hugged with those bionic arms. It was truly a miracle.

God always has another miracle. Claim it!

Lord, thank you for giving inventors and prosthetists the ability to copy your work in making the human body. May we never take the birth of a healthy baby with all body parts for granted. Amen.

Spiritual Healing

Julia was stricken with the dreaded disease dermatomyositis, which strikes only 1 in 300,000 persons. It left her with excruciating pain in all of her muscles, joints, connective tissue, and skin. She had a rash on her upper eyelids and growths on her fingers, knuckles, elbows, and knees. Her scalp was irritated, and her hair was coming out in patches. In other words, she was a mess! But Julia did not despair. She claimed the Word of God, which said, "By His stripes we are healed" (Isaiah 53:5b NKJV). She kept expressing the belief that healing is ready when we are. As soon as we believe it, we receive it.

Of course, everyone thought she was crazy. Her friends looked at her and told her that she could not walk and that her face and limbs were swollen and inflamed. How could she claim healing when there was no evidence of it? Yet Julia told them that she was spiritually healed, but the physical manifestation of that healing might take a little longer.

Julia ignored those who did not believe in her healing. She even ignored the doctors who said that there was no cure for her disease and that there was rarely remission in adults. She was told that she had to prepare for the destruction of her major organs, but she refused to let fear overwhelm her. She started meditating on healing scriptures. She found Psalm 103 most comforting, especially the words, "Bless the LORD ... who heals all your diseases" (vv. 2-3 NRSV). Then she remembered the words of Jesus when he said that if you believe in your heart and do not doubt, you can tell a mountain to move, and it will move (Mark 11:23). Julia told the mountain of disease that had engulfed her body to move, and, miraculously, it moved! Her miracle of spiritual healing became a physical healing because of her faith.

God always has another miracle. Claim it!

Lord, give me faith to move the mountains in my life. Amen.

The Miracle Touch

Pastor Allen Tanner frequently works with the chaplain at the Department of Corrections, and he was asked to visit with an inmate who had AIDS and was told that he had approximately three weeks to live. Finding the patient in a semi-comatose state, Allen decided to spend his time telling the young man a biblical story of healing. The story he chose was that of the woman with the issue of blood (Mark 5:25-34).

Allen told how the woman was considered unclean because

of her bleeding, but she persevered to touch the hem of Jesus' garment, believing that the act of touching would heal her. He encouraged the young man to visualize touching Jesus and being made well. He emphasized the fact that the woman had to push and even crawl through the crowd just to get close enough to touch Jesus' hem. She had no hope of being able to actually touch him, but she believed that there was enough healing power for her in his hem. Allen explained to the young man that, in like manner, he would have to make his journey toward wholeness alone. He would have to push through his troubled mind and find his way to the healing touch that only Jesus could provide.

Obviously, the young man accepted Allen's challenge, for within twenty-four hours he was sitting up and feeling better. He was told that one-third of the AIDS virus had vanished from his body. With this news, Allen knew that eventually all of the virus would vanish, for it was his firm belief that God never leaves a job unfinished. Sure enough, over the next two days, the final two-thirds of the virus vanished.

The young man returned to prison, witnessing to his healing that had come through visualizing himself touching the hem of Jesus' garment. He is a living testimony to the miracle power of the living Lord.

God always has another miracle. Claim it!

God, make me a witness to your miracle power. Amen.

The Miracle Spot

It was a Wednesday morning, and as Martha was getting ready to shower for work, she noticed a spot on her nightgown. Closely checking her body and the place where the spot appeared, she noticed that there was a discharge coming from her breast, which she knew was not normal. She decided that going to work would have to wait; she believed that that spot was a sign from God that she needed to proceed immediately to the emergency room.

Upon arriving at the hospital, she was given several tests and a mammogram. It was finally determined that she had fatty cancerous tissue in the lower portion of one of her breasts. A total mastectomy was recommended. Martha took this news in stride. She was not afraid, for she knew that God was with her. Because of the spot that God had caused her to notice, she would soon be cancer free. Although Martha knew that her doctor expected her to be upset, she explained that God was with her and would be with both of them throughout the procedure she was to undergo. Martha believed that her response to her cancer provided an opportunity to witness to her faith.

Within two days of seeing the discharge, Martha had surgery. While in the recovery room, she automatically felt for her breast. It had been removed, along with the cancer, but she was alive and able to praise God for her life-threatening discovery. Her doctor informed her that chemotherapy would not be necessary, so she would not have to worry about losing her hair. She thought to herself, "God is good all of the time. He has saved my life and my hair."

Martha has come to think of that spot as a miracle, for she knows that God is in the miracle business and that he always has another one. Claim it!

Lord, make us aware of the signs you provide to help medical personnel save our lives. Amen.

The Miracle Vow

Kim and Krickitt Carpenter had been married only two months. They were looking forward to celebrating their first Thanksgiving as a married couple. While driving to Krickitt's parents' home, they had a terrible automobile accident. Both Kim and Krickitt were seriously injured, but Krickitt was not expected to recover. She was airlifted to the nearest hospital, and her husband followed by ground transportation.

When Kim reached the hospital, he was told that his wife was in a coma and was beyond medical help. He knew that even if she was beyond medical help, she was not beyond God's help. He began to pray for the miracle cure he knew that she needed.

The doctor gave Krickitt's watch and wedding ring to Kim. As he held them, he remembered the vow he had made just two months earlier: "For better, for worse ... in sickness and in health." He had promised; he had made a vow, and he would pray her through this coma.

Krickitt was in the coma for two weeks. When she recovered, her long-term memory was intact. However, she did not remember anything that had happened in the past two years. She did not know she was married and did not recognize her husband. Kim could have walked away, but he remembered his vow and promised to stay with her and win her love all over again.

Krickitt fell in love with Kim a second time, married him again wearing the same wedding dress, and later gave birth to their first child. Kim was faithful to his vow, and a miracle resulted.

God always has another miracle. Claim it!

Lord, help us be faithful to the vows and promises we make. Amen.

The Miracle of Determination

Adrienne was working in a downtown law office. Although she had been accepted to a prestigious law school, she had decided to work for a year before enrolling. While on her way to work one morning, she was hit by a car. The blow was so severe, and her body appeared to be so broken, that everyone who saw the accident assumed she was dead. But those observers did not know Adrienne and the spirit of determination she possessed.

Rushed by ambulance to the hospital, Adrienne was

stabilized and given excellent care around the clock. It appeared that the emergency room staff knew that Adrienne had a dream to realize, and they did not want to let her down. She had already experienced her first miracle; she had survived the accident.

Everyone who knew Adrienne prayed for her recovery. They knew that she would have a difficult time, and they were not sure if she would ever walk again. After several months, Adrienne was released from the hospital in a wheelchair. She could not walk, but her spirit of determination had not faltered.

Adrienne entered law school in a wheelchair, for whether she could walk or not, she needed to get on with the realization of her dream. In the midst of her studies and new environment, she continued her therapy. Adrienne knew that learning to walk again would require hard work, and she was determined. Finally she was strong enough to use crutches, but they just kept getting in the way of her dream; that dream did not include crutches. She prayed to be able to put those crutches down, and one day she did. She experienced her second miracle when she walked on her own!

Adrienne finished her first year of law school and got a job working as an intern in a judge's office in a large city. Not only had she survived the accident and learned to walk again, but she also had excelled because she was determined to realize her dream.

God always has another miracle. Claim it!

Lord, instill in us the kind of determination that leads to miraculous results. Amen.

FAITH

I tell you the truth, if you have faith as small as a mustard seed,
you can say to this mountain, "Move from here to there" and it will move.
Nothing will be impossible for you.

—Matthew 17:20

Trusting God

Marcy lived in a cold climate, and she used coal to heat her house. As the weather worsened, she knew that it was time to purchase coal; but after counting her money, she did not have enough money to buy both coal and food for her family. She had always trusted God to supply her needs. So, when she felt led to ask her friend to lend her the money, she made the phone call. Her friend agreed to lend her the money, and Marcy ordered the coal.

Coal was only delivered once a month, and it was time for the delivery. Marcy went to her friend's house to get the money. When she arrived, she was informed that her friend's children needed the money and there would not be enough for Marcy's coal. Marcy returned home to wait for the coal to be delivered. She did not know what she would say to the deliveryman or how she would pay for the coal, so she just started praying and trusting that God would somehow provide.

While she was waiting, the mail came. In with the mail was a note with cash from a person to whom she had loaned money many months earlier. She had forgotten that she had never been repaid. Although the note contained an apology for the lateness in repaying the debt, Marcy thought to herself, "This money is not late; it is right on time."

Marcy began to praise God for answering her prayer, and she noted that God had been very specific. If the money owed her had been sent in the form of a check, she still would not have been able to pay for the coal. Although she knew that it was not wise to send cash in the mail, she was grateful that, this time, cash had been sent.

Marcy is a firm believer that God always has another miracle, and she claimed hers. What about you? Are you claiming your miracle today?

Lord, I know that you supply all that we need, and I thank you that I can stand on your promises. Amen.

The Miracle of Faith

Nineteen years ago when Andrew Curry was given the grim news that he had cancer and had only six months to live, he was devastated. He lamented the fact that he would not live to see his beloved daughter graduate from high school or go to college. He would not have the opportunity to give her away in marriage or become a doting grandfather when she had children. He would miss so much of life.

Andy recited this litany of blessings that he would miss to me and to my husband, his pastor. Although I tried to offer words of comfort, I accepted the doctor's diagnosis and tried to help Andy rejoice in the good life he had already experienced with his loving wife and beautiful daughter. My husband did not accept the doctor's prediction. He said that the doctor was not in charge; God was. He told Andy that if he had faith and believed that he would live to see all of the things he wanted to, he could. But Andy doubted. His pastor did not. His pastor finally said, "If you don't have enough faith to believe that you will live to see these things come to pass, then live on my faith—because I believe it."

Andy believed in his pastor and accepted his gift of faith. With faith and determination, he lived nineteen years after his initial diagnosis. He saw his daughter graduate from high school and college. He proudly walked her down the aisle at her wedding, and he bounced his grandson on his knee. He did all the things he wanted to do. His life was complete. He finished his course, for he had experienced his miracle of faith.

Do you have miracle-making faith? My husband does. He knows that God always has another miracle. All we have to do is claim it!

Lord, give us that mustard seed faith that can move mountains. Amen.

The Miraculous Request

Monica and her infant great-grandson were rushed to the hospital on the same day and at the same time. They were both in extremely critical condition, suffering from the same condition—congestive heart failure. The prognosis was not good. It was discovered that the infant, who was only four months old, was missing a chamber of his heart. He needed immediate heart surgery, after which he would be placed on a ventilator. Monica, on the other hand, though feeble, was holding on to life with a strong sense of determination. It seemed ironic that the infant was fighting to live while his great-grandmother was refusing to die.

After a few days, the doctors told the family that neither Monica nor the infant would survive. Monica's daughter went to Monica with a request. She asked Monica to go to the Father and ask him to save the baby's life. It just might be possible that Monica could do in heaven what she could not do on earth.

Shortly after the request had been made, Monica let go of her earthly life. The next morning, her great-grandson was taken off the ventilator and lived. He has subsequently had five open-heart surgeries, but he has survived.

I wonder what request Monica made when she met the Father. It was surely a miraculous one.

God always has another miracle. Claim it!

Holy Father, we know you understand our longing to save others, for you gave your Son for us all. Thank you. Amen.

The Registration Miracle

Years ago there was no online registration for college classes. Students had to stand in line and patiently wait to register for classes. Sometimes when they finally got to the head of the line, the classes for which they wanted to register were already filled. And, of course, they had to have all of their money for registration with them.

Maynell, Helen, and Ora were roommates at a university many years ago. Although Helen and Ora had their money for registration, Maynell was short. Nevertheless, all three students got in the long line to register. Ora and Helen asked Maynell how she intended to pay for her registration. Maynell said that she did not know, but she believed that by the time she got to the head of the line, she would have her money.

Of course, neither Helen nor Ora believed her, but they did not say anything about it. They just decided that she would find out that money does not grow on trees. They also did not want her to lose faith if she really believed that the money would miraculously appear.

The girls were in line almost an hour, but it was finally their turn to register. No one had approached them and given Maynell the money she needed, but Maynell stayed in line. Helen was the first to register, and she was surprised to discover that she had extra money in her account. Knowing that she did not need it, she asked if she could transfer it to Maynell. She was told that she could, and it was exactly the amount that Maynell needed to complete her registration.

After Maynell and Ora had completed their registrations, Maynell said, "I told you I would have the money by the time I registered." And she did. It was a miracle.

God always has another miracle. Claim it!

Lord, give us the faith that knows you will supply our every need. We just need that mustard seed faith. Amen.

The Miracle of Spirit

In her book *The Ultimate Flight: In Search of Mike* (Colorado Springs, Colo.: Word Press, 1996), Martha Chamberlain tells the story of a family friend named Mike who had always wanted to be a Navy pilot. His dream was realized, and he loved flying. He was a fine Christian gentleman who was looking forward to a Christ-centered marriage when tragedy occurred. His plane never returned from a routine flight.

Both Mike and the captain with whom he was flying were listed as missing, and the plane was presumed to have crashed. There was an initial investigation, but the plane was not found. Although the mishap was labeled "pilot error," that designation was unacceptable to the families and friends of both men. The Navy was unwilling to investigate further and discouraged all others from doing so, as well. However, the families and friends would not be discouraged. They needed the peace of knowing the truth about what had occurred. Two years after the mishap, the remains of the plane were discovered, and, eventually, bone fragments were identified as belonging to the two men.

In her book, Mrs. Chamberlain records how she discovered who Mike was and where he was. She discovered who he was first. She found friends and family who described his spirit and his Christian commitment, and she saw his spirit live in those who loved him. She also found where he was. Although his body fragments were at the foot of the mountain into which he had crashed, his spirit was alive with his Savior.

When Christians die, their spirits live on. They surround us with their love and they bless us with their presence. They are immortal, for they live in us. It is a miracle!

God always has another miracle. Claim it!

Lord, thank you for the gift of the Holy Spirit. We have also received the gift of the spirit of those who have died in Christ, and for that miracle we are grateful. Amen.

The Miracle Release

My mother's name was Louise B. Lindsay, and she was ninety-six years old. She had been saying that she was tired for several months, and she had been telling me that she was going home. I kept advising her to rest, and I tried to convince her that she *was* at home.

One month before her death, she fell and cut her head. It appeared that she had suffered several ministrokes, and her health rapidly declined. She was hospitalized and given a number of tests. While in the hospital, she fell again and cut her head in a different place. When the doctors ordered more tests, she looked at me and said, "No! God has done all he is going to do." With those words, she stopped eating and began to sleep more.

The doctors advised me to listen to her. She knew it was time to be released. I was resisting because she was my mother and I wanted to keep her with me forever. Logically, I knew that my wish was not possible, so I found a beautiful hospice where she could spend her final days. During those last days, she did what she had done all of her life: she quoted scripture. She often said, "Praise ye the LORD . . . ; for he is good: for his mercy endureth for ever" (Psalm 106:1 KJV). Then she would say, "I will lift up mine eyes unto the hills, from whence cometh my help. My help cometh from the LORD, which made heaven and earth" (Psalm 121:1-2 KJV). That verse would be followed by, "The LORD is my light and my salvation" (Psalm 27:1a), and then she would recite the Twenty-third Psalm in its entirety. Sometimes we said that psalm as a litany. She would say one verse, and I would say the next.

On October 29, I prayed with her for the miracle of release. She died while those gathered around her bed were praying. She smiled. She had experienced her miracle.

God always has another miracle. Claim it!

Lord, death is the bridge that leads to eternal life. Grant us safe crossing in Jesus. Amen.

VISION

Where there is no vision, the people perish.
                                              —Proverbs 29:18 (KJV)

A Miracle Resolution

When each new year begins, I wonder how many of us make new year's resolutions. Do we resolve to lose weight, attend church more regularly, read our Bibles more faithfully, or spend more time with our families? Perhaps we resolve to learn how to cook or how to use the computer or how to knit. We might even resolve to read a specific number of books during the year. No matter what we resolve, by March, most of us have forgotten all about our resolutions or have decided that whatever they were, they were not high on our list of priorities.

Consider an alterative to new year's resolutions. Why not begin the next year by making new day's resolutions? Instead of making resolutions for the whole year, just make resolutions for one day. Then our resolution to lose weight would take this form: I will not eat or drink anything sweet today. Our resolution to attend church more regularly would result in deciding each day whether or not to attend a Bible study, meeting, or worship service. We would resolve each day to read our Bibles and to spend an hour more with our families. We might even resolve to sign up for that cooking, computer, or knitting class. We would make our resolutions on a daily basis, and we would have much better success in keeping them.

Alcoholics Anonymous and Gamblers Anonymous have practiced this principle for years. Just take one day at a time. Each day we should strive to be more like Jesus. Each day we should resolve to do some good or kind act for someone else. Each day we should seek to make a positive difference in someone's life. Keeping our daily resolutions would truly be a miracle.

Remember that God always has another miracle. Claim it!

Lord, help me this day make and keep a resolution that demonstrates my Christian discipleship. Amen.

An Easter Miracle

What would a real Easter miracle look like? Would it be a new bonnet, dress, or suit? Would it be a new pair of shoes, a shirt, or a tie? Would it be an Easter play or speech? Would it be watching a movie about Jesus Christ on the big screen? Would it even be a sunrise service? Of course not!

Somehow we have gotten the real Easter miracle mixed up with its earthly commercialism. We spend money we do not have to buy the latest fashions to usher in spring properly. We insist that our children, who have not even regularly attended Sunday school, be given Easter speeches so that we can admire them and brag about how much they have learned. We discuss how moved we were by a depiction on the stage or big screen of Christ's suffering and death, but where is the Easter miracle?

Though new clothes remind us that spring has come, bringing with it new life in our yards and gardens, and though having our children learn Easter speeches helps them fight the fear of speaking before an audience, and though watching a play or movie depicting Christ being beaten and crucified may remind us of the great debt we owe, none of this represents the Easter miracle.

It would be a miracle if, as we donned new clothes, we also donned a new life. It would be a miracle if we vowed to live as peacemakers who reflect our role as children of God. It would be a miracle if we knew and used new Bible verses in our lives—not just for Easter speeches that are soon forgotten. It would be a miracle if we lived a life of thanksgiving to Christ for the suffering he endured so that we might have eternal life. Perhaps reorienting our thinking about and our response to the Resurrection would truly be an Easter miracle.

God always has another miracle. Claim it!

Lord, thank you for the miraculous gift of eternal life. May we celebrate your gift not only on our holiest of days—on the day of the Resurrection—but also every day. Amen.

Christmas Every Day

For many years I was a volunteer at the children's division of Grady Memorial Hospital in Atlanta, Georgia. Somehow I always became distressed as Christmas approached. It seemed that every individual, service organization, neighborhood club, and church thought that it would be wonderful to donate toys and food to the sick children. Subsequently, we at the hospital were bombarded with donations. We had no place to store all the donations, and all the children who were in the hospital went home with more than they could carry.

I suppose you wonder why this situation distressed me, but I always wondered why everyone decided that Christmas was the only time that children needed toys and attention. I just wished that some groups would bring toys in March or July or October. I wanted to let them know that the children who were hospitalized in those months would have loved to have some of those toys. I even heard some children saying that they hoped they would get sick near Christmas because there were always lots of gifts for children who were in the hospital then.

I never will forget one little girl who was hospitalized a week before Christmas. She was in the activity room when a box of beautiful dolls was delivered. She saw the dolls and really wanted one. She asked if they were for Christmas, and I told her that they would be given to the children on Christmas morning. The little girl just beamed knowing that she would be receiving one of those beautiful dolls, but her doctor told her mother that she could go home two days before Christmas. Suddenly the child got sick. She told the doctor that she had lots of aches and pains. She just had to stay in the hospital until Christmas. I knew what the situation really was and gave her one of the dolls. Of course, she miraculously recovered.

Although her recovery wasn't a miracle, it made me think of the miracle that would result if we truly celebrated Christmas every day. What if we adopted the spirit of giving all year long? What if we periodically visited hospitals and took toys to the children? That would truly be a miracle.

God always has another miracle. Claim it!

Lord, help me remember to celebrate your birth and the spirit of love it brings every day. Amen.

The Miraculous Gift

When I am suddenly made aware of the sin that daily abounds in our world, I believe we need a miracle. The miracle that we need is the one Jesus most often employed. It is the miraculous gift of healing. We need to be healed so that we do not enter a sacred sanctuary and make it a place of murder. We need to be healed so that we do not leave a two-year-old child alone for almost three weeks without providing food, water, and basic care. We need healing so that we do not deposit our elders in nursing homes and never visit them. We need healing so that we can recover from the sick and selfish society we have become. We need the miraculous gift of healing that only comes with salvation. Come, Lord Jesus.

What can we do to receive this miracle of healing salvation?

Jesus gave us the answer. We must repent. We must turn from our wicked ways and return to God. Through the ages, God's people have been disobedient to the law. They have suffered exile, bondage, persecution, and death. God sent prophet after prophet with the same message of repentance, but the people did not listen. Finally, God sent his Son, Jesus, the Christ. I wonder if we are prepared to receive him and the salvation he brings.

Will we listen to his message? Will we seek the healing that only he can give? Will we turn from our wicked ways? Will we be born again? If we will, we will experience the real miracle of his birth, and I believe in miracles.

Remember that God always has another miracle. Claim it!

Lord, thank you for the great gift of your Son. Thank you for the healing that only he can bring into our lives. Amen.

The Final Miracle

My ninety-two-year-old aunt died a few years ago. Although my aunt had lived a full and active life, her last days were plagued with health problems. She had diabetes, kidney failure, heart failure, and pneumonia. Her breathing was labored, and her glands were swollen to the point that it was difficult for her to swallow. Yet, my relatives wanted her to hang on. They begged the doctors to do all they could to prolong her life. They were unwilling to let her go.

I wonder why we try to keep our loved ones past the time that their physical bodies can support their existence. It appears that one who has lived ninety-two years ought to be ready to move from this earthly life to life eternal. Our earthly bodies do wear out. They become fragile and function less efficiently, and we find it more difficult to do the things we used to do with ease. God did not intend for us to live in these earthly bodies forever. These bodies were created to deteriorate.

No matter how much our physical bodies deteriorate, we, as Christians, have hope. We need not be discouraged regarding our earthly vessels, because there is a final miracle, the miracle of eternal life. However, this miracle is reserved for those who have received salvation. When we and our loved ones have lived our lives in the knowledge of God and have accepted the salvation offered by our Savior, we ought to rejoice when it is time for our final miracle.

What a blessing it is to let go, to give up this earthly dwelling and be welcomed into the arms of the Savior. This is indeed the final miracle, the blessing of all blessings, the glorious gift of eternal life.

God always has another miracle. Claim it!

Lord, I want to be ready when it is time for me to receive my final miracle. Amen.